Sentences

from

the

Archive

Sentences from the Archive
Recent Work Press
Canberra, Australia

Copyright © Jen Webb, 2016

National Library of Australia
Cataloguing-in-Publication entry.

Webb, Jen
Sentences from the Archive/ Jen Webb
ISBN:9780995353800 (paperback)
Australian Poetry

All rights reserved. This book is copyright. Except for private study,
research, criticism or reviews as permitted under the Copyright Act,
no part of this book may be reproduced, stored in a retrieval system, or
transmitted in any form by any means without prior written permission.
Enquiries should be addressed to the publisher.

Cover illustration: Sunlight Yarns steel crochet hooks (1912) [modified],
by Natalia Wilson, 2012 reproduced under Creative Commons
Attribution-Share Alike 2.0 licence

Cover design: Recent Work Press
Set in Walbaum by Recent Work Press

recentworkpress.com

Sentences

from

the

Archive

Jen Webb

Contents

Outside the orchard	1
Tarte au citron	2
The heart of the sea	3
Dès que le soleil	7
Waiting for the phone to ring	11
On the road	14
Looking for America	16
Finding America	17
Digging up the past	18
In the eye of the storm	19
For the record	20
Writing the past	22
The minutes of the meeting	23
Inside the archive	24
No stories please	26
Elegy	27
Writing the map	31
1973	38
Starting over	39
What happened that night	40
Keeping the record straight	41
En route	42
Icarus	43
Waiting for the bus	44
Drops in time	52
Da capo	53
Afterword	54

Outside the orchard

Green apples, so rich a crop we wasted them, bowling them on weekend afternoons, knocking them for six. Dark macrocarpa trees line the avenue. You driving home between the trees, late again but welcome all the same. I sketched you, later, as you slept, filling the pages of my notebook with your hand, your arm, the line of your jaw. I peeled apples and sliced them fingernail-deep, waking you with their scent. The astringent bite. Fluid in the mouth. Green skin, spiraling a green S across the lawn.

Tarte au citron

All through those years we breakfasted on grapefruits picked warm that morning, squeezed our own limes into lunchtime gin, ate cheese with apples that tasted of the sun. You ate your oranges in the garden—it's an inelegant sight, you said—and you rolled your sleeves to your elbows, dug your thumbs into the fruit and drank down the juice that sprayed and squirted and ran down your chin. Afterward, the sweetness still on your skin, you would look at me, lubricious, and I would lean into you, hungry as a flame. The babies came, and the locals laughed at my fecundity, and I blamed the fruit. I hear stories of the orchard, sometimes, and of its fate. Never go back, they say. I never have.

The heart of the sea

'We are kids, we have broken hearts, we have little hearts, we come here to get our wishes, but here is not our wishes.'
(child refugee on Nauru; Sydney Morning Herald, *11 August 2016, p.7)*

I

We had weeks at sea, travelling between cyclone season and the dry. We watched something advancing toward us, across the screen of the sky. At first I thought it grey, but someone said no, it's green, and someone else thought gold. We could never agree on the colour, but what difference does a shade make? The navy arrived in fast boats, urging us to board, guaranteeing our lives. (But we had seen the news. We know where safe passage ends: an unstable tent, our children stacked like stones to build a wall.) No way! we said. We cut the cables, refused to wave goodbye, got under way. Tonight we wait, hand in hand, standing on the deck. In the distance we see it draw nearer. I think that it's a rainstorm, but someone says no, it's angels. Someone else says it is the herald of our end. What difference can it make? If we live, what stories will we tell? We wait. Taking our chance.

II

Our bodies, drifting. The sky, drifting. The boats weaving between us, oblivious. Salt in our mouths, in our eyes. We swam until we were tired, and then we drifted again. Our arms remember, our legs, our skin. The sea. Our first home and our last.

III

An amplified heartbeat. A spider web wrapping the ward, black silk, tender knots, a nurse's touch. Outside children are calling, their voices thin in winter air. The sea breathes against the wharf. People keep coming, hauling their bags and their elderly to the shore.

IV

What I remember is the colour of the sea. Its voice as it summoned me, its touch when I leaned across the rail. The sea, stroking my hair, slipping down my shirt, reaching inside me. It took my little heart, and when I cried out NO it covered my mouth. When I woke again, I had the heart of the sea in my breast. A different beat. Cold blood. Now the boat is gone, and my love is gone; the sun has burned away the heart of the sea, turned it back to salt. I drift at the edge of the shore, without a heart, listening for your voice. Here is not my wishes. No one any longer calls my name.

Dès que le soleil

I

You appear in my notebooks as M. A thin disguise for those who knew us, but it pleases me to keep you in the shadows. I avoid you these days, just as I avoid the sun. The tree we planted casts a staggered shade, paints leaves on my skin. I sprawl beneath it, pour myself some wine, and when you call me I leave the phone to ring.

Dès que le soleil ('When the sun'): aria from Act III of Georges Bizet's The Pearl Fishers.

II

Although it wasn't much of a path, we followed it, tiptoeing step by step up its battered stones. In the shadowed parts you flared up, burning light into corners, knocking away the cobwebs. When the path led under the road we crouched there, silent, reading the graffiti on the walls, while planes crisscrossed above us, stitching up the sky. When you reached for my hand I held you like a star. When you kissed me I thought of light. Of sealing the wound. Of choosing why not over why.

III

You come to me, wrapped, the gift I've been waiting for: touch me. I come to you, wrapped, my skin silk on yours, the wind twitches and we sway in our shrouds. Find the rhythm. I touch you, you groan. Don't look down, the building is high, the ground is hard, if we lose faith we will fall, we will not fall.

IV

Your ridiculous hair, my spray-on dress, my blood, your sunsets. You, who can't distinguish green from blue; you, who calls orange red: you have claimed this hour. When the sun begins its fall you open the windows, belt out the aria from *The Pearl Fishers*, and the sun crash-lands behind the Brindabellas, and you sing on. The evening rises to meet us, and I have almost forgiven you. Three streets over there's a siren calling off-key, B flat to your C, and if memory could speak it would say *lock it in, Eddie, lock it in*.

Waiting for the phone to ring

I

Dark rain. We swivel, midstride, avoiding an impact with something coming toward us in the wrong lane. Flick the lights down low because the moon looks so distressed. You are fretting about the report that is overdue and unprepared. I am waiting for the doctor to call. Something is coming toward us, fast, in the wrong lane. Or is it just the rain?

II

There is something amiss. Mice in the pantry. Something dead in the walls. You spray perfume, burn incense, wash the floors with vinegar. The air smells of fish hooks and ice. Last night I found you standing, your face to the wall, sponge and spray bottle in hand. I think you were weeping, but it may just have been the bleach in the air. Open the windows, dearest, spread out your wings. Death comes and goes like the weather. Wait long enough and it will be your turn, and mine.

III

When the doors close against you. When your feet forget to walk. You remember nothing about the weeks and years before, sense has become not-sense, grief a shadow in the corners of your day. Before the lights go out, before the walls close in on you, call me. You know it's on its way. You know it can't be outrun. Keep your head down. Before the last chance reaches you, call me. I'll find you if I can.

On the road

I

We drive all day, past little towns no longer on the highway, where the fish-and-chip lady each day sets out her fillets of fish and tubs of batter, her freshly rinsed lettuce, her chipped potatoes, and she heats the vats of oil, and turns on the extractor fan, and flips the sign to open, and waits through another long day when only the temporary road crew front up for lunch and the bills are mounting and she's not sure how long she can struggle on but if not this, what will she do with herself, what could anyone do?

II

The rubber has hit the road, the chips are down, the cavalry haven't called, and the elbow of the hills is empty. Across the plain the storm is coming. We look at each other and know that the enemy is upon us, but what the fuck, we're still alive. Like ET, our fingers stretch across the abyss: only connect. You say, *If I knew now what I knew then*; I say, *And vice versa*; and we laugh, despite. We are catching our breath and letting it go, and catching it again, before it falls. Remember that time we stood on the very top of the mountain and did not fall? Remember when you held me and all I did was laugh? Surely we can find our way through this mess too? The dollar has sunk to an historic low and the DAX is stumbling. I will jam splinters under my nails, poke laser beams at my eyes: anything to wake myself up. You are losing your faith, I am scouring the evidence. Surely someone will open a door for us? Surely we will find a way through?

Looking for America

Instead of time you give me facts: 'a third of America travels this road each day'; 'one Michael Baker designed the Beltway'; 'Hanover Street is a parking lot'. The cars are nose to tail, elephants in a circus, hamsters in a wheel. You keep talking. You love spending time at the farm but no one knows you out there; in the city, everyone says *Hi! How you doing?* When the traffic stops, we stop, and pull onto the shoulder to kill time. *Is this smart*, I ask, when you kiss me. You don't reply. You crack the whiskey and we pass the bottle back and forth. *We'll never make it to Baltimore at this rate*, I say, and you reach for me. Too intimate, too soon. I'm not really sure that this is safe.

Finding America

Everything changed in a beat: you can see it in the shock the ghost still carries on his face. The guns he faced are locked in museums now, and the grass is struggling up through bones between the worried trees, and light falls like shutters. You smell the old terror, the stench of fire. Duck your head, cover your eyes. You are there. You were never there. When I tap your arm the ghost fades into the shadow between two trees. *Come on*; and we stand up, between the skeletons of lost lives, and make our way back to the crest of the hill, to the open lawn beyond the haunted woods, to the renovated home. We bring with us small treasures we have found between the press of boots, the fired soil, the tracks of heavy guns. I have the arm of a little doll, you carry the shards of someone's cup. This is not my history, this is not my war. The trees have seen it all before and the dread of it returns to shudder them, there where they stand, on the banks of the river of America.

Digging up the past

She knew it would end like this: the sharp erosion; rain that will not fall; one walk too many in shoes that don't fit. There's a twice-filled grave, just beyond the wall. There's that bottle you ought to refuse but don't. There's the wine that costs too much. Hold fresh-dug earth in your hand: breathe in its chthonic scent. If you listen closely, you will hear the whispers of worms as they flake the soil. Don't try to parse its meaning. Meaning doesn't mean the way it did when we were kids, when words came piled in paper cones, when it smelt of popcorn and joy. Those days are gone, darling. Now it's ashes, and salt.

In the eye of the storm

Words fail. You return to the state you left so long ago when the only knowledge you had was colour and shape, movements and sounds. Sensation, in other words: only that makes sense right now. The wind is shouting to be heard above the racket of buildings crying out in complaint. A bus whips past, drenching you. Reduced as you are to stutter, you can't expostulate. It's all right: wordless, you become innocence. The wind takes your umbrella and lifts you off the pavement. One exquisite moment of flight, and then the boom swings the other way, and knocks you down. Icon and symbol may have deserted you, but index still packs a punch.

For the record

I

Born on the first day of the month, in the last month of the year, as the cyclones begin to wake, stretching, gathering strength, and then look our way: contemplatively. Born between the coffee and the cake, while the nurses stretched in their station, hoping someone would rub away their aches. Another everyday miracle: no less miracle for that. As your parents stretch their tired arms, as they check their charts and chart a new course, as they weigh anchor, you begin to wake, stretching, gathering strength. We will keep you our secret. Refer to you only as Q.

II

All those nights. The muted lamp in the other room. Your father sleeping as I reach for the handrails, groaning myself upright. Your little mouth opens and closes as the milk queues up in my breasts. In your room it is soft sounds; outside the house, moreporks call; across the hall your sister cries out in her sleep: the cat strolls by, pauses to look in our door, heads for her cot. No more sleepwalking into history, no more private nights. You look at me, and smile, your mouth curving around my nipple. No more looking over my shoulder. The night is entirely silent. There's just the stutter of my heart, trying out the rhythms that fit your own.

Writing the past

Slipstreaming between cities and lovers, spilling grapes from my sleeves so the birds follow me like acolytes, I light the candles of your memory. Mice collect the melting wax and carry it away, slipping between the wainscot and the wall. You again: your 'unbearable' beauty, your 'remarkably' low price. I have bought you in a hundred ways, crumbled you between my fingers, called the city's pigeons to feed from my outstretched hands. Let me make amends: I'll clip my own wings and fly in spirals, drawing closer with every turn, then land too hard, breaking all my small bones, making amends, a fluttered bird.

The minutes of the meeting

There's always an older man who is angry about everything. He wears a beard and, often, a bowtie. The fruit platter will be only a whole pineapple and no knife. The coffee will be cold. No windows, no screens. There will be no phone calls, no leaving the room, till the agenda is done. And then a cat strolls in through the cracked-open door, a lizard dangling from its mouth. Three people shout, several coo, someone cracks a joke. That woman who always speaks so intensely is insisting that silver is best, it goes with everything. Then she sees the cat. The minutes secretary hesitates: floored, flawed. A memory of blood on the walls, of lost socks trying to find their way back home. Someone is touching someone too intimately. The agenda is forgotten. The cat places its catch neatly at the head of the table, and leaves the room. It's not a no, but it is the opposite of yes.

Inside the archive

I

The radio clicks on and now it's good morning in Perth, where it has just hit six o'clock. In Brisbane it's mid morning and rain is falling. From his eyrie he looks down to the river; which has changed its mind about the city; which is looking for the off-ramp. He should eat something. Rain is falling, clouds building a berm against the cyclone that is still days away. He can't remember for the moment why he isn't home; then it comes back to him. Last chance. It is six a.m. in Perth. No one is calling his phone; the rain is still falling.

II

He begins the small duties that put a lid on the day: the washing and tidying of kitchen and self; the shutting of the windows, the turning of the keys. The phone rings briefly, then stops; his house pauses, a moment's silence for the incompleteness of things. A cat cries at the door to be let in. He would cry too, but there is no one to open the door, no cushion where he can curl himself, and sleep.

No stories please

Low moon tonight. It scrapes a new wound against the ridge of the sky. We wander up and down the aisles. The avocados are too hard, or too soft. Tomatoes are bright. Cheese is marked down. In the aisle the man ahead of us is buying tulips, and chocolates, and cream. We could speculate on his story, on who he needs to please, but what purpose would it serve? The dog is waiting outside. As I unchain him, you look up and see a gold star. It's not good luck or bad, you say. It simply is. Minutes later I look up and the star has become a helicopter, patrolling the streets. We walk home, hand in hand. We are trying so hard. Don't we deserve a prize?

Elegy

I

What happens afterward is that you look, and keep looking. Something cold has burrowed under your skin. An emptiness. You find a pebble in your hand, but don't remember selecting it. Time lurches back, and like a fool balloon it spirals madly across the room. You will never see him again. You will look, and keep looking, but he has gone and taken with him all his stories, all his self, and all you can do is hold that pebble in your hand, hold it and breathe as the world shudders and then fires back into life, and steadies, and the passengers breathe more easily, and everything goes on as though nothing has happened at all.

II

After the funeral we tidied up his life. A brother sourced packing crates, a sister found a skip. Our aunt brought pots of soup and her son designed a schedule. My niece unearthed a typewriter from among the mould and the mice, and wiped it down, and played it, her pianist's fingers at the keys, the bass rumble of platen, the treble bell, a sweet percussion, the typewriter finding its voice.

III

The capsicum left too long in the fridge, the carrots left too long in the fridge, the potatoes that have grown eyes, the onions with their rotten cores, the love I never gave you. Check the bread for mould, think of starving children, eat up all the scraps. The garden calls out, and I move between its beds, and the plants lean against me, intimate friends. They stroke their leaves across my skin and I stroke them too. These days I take affection wherever I can find it.

IV

It was a long time coming, but you got there in the end. Four times already you'd had the last rites, an old comfort. On the last time you did not join in. Funerals should be held in the rain, but yours will be in brilliant sun. We will dig your grave between the frangipani trees, on the slopes outside the city, where the old gum trees cast an afternoon shade. Every spring will be new leaf, dense flowers. We will not mourn you long.

Writing the map

'If one does not know to which port one is sailing, no wind is favourable.' (Seneca)

I

The 'following wind'. Sailors love it. Men scrabble among the ropes, hauling sails back to jib. A pocket handkerchief, it puffs out its cheeks and it's *whee!*, the wind at your back, the wind in your hair, check the sextant and yes, that's the way home. Isn't it? Away we go, over the surface of the sea, until someone checks the charts and it's *wrong-way-Roger*, too late to tack into the by-now-howling gale, we are set on our path, and the sea has teamed up with the wind and is careening us towards what looks like *oh god* rocks.

II

Fish hooks; the scent of salt; the long days on the edge of Africa, you casting your line, me watching the sea anemones open and close. When I was a child, with no feeling for flowers or fish, I trailed my fingers through their Mardi Gras fronds. The incongruous clamp against my skin. Them tasting me. They spat me out, and stretched out again into the sea, on the hunt. Later that day you packed up sinkers and hooks, tangles of line, your killing blade. The unused bait you threw into the sea. Took my hand in your own, despite slime and scale. When you kissed me, I tasted rust and stale blood.

III

You hauled the hook from that fish, and thrust it into the creel, and as we watched it wrestled itself over the brim and away. We followed it, respectfully. It moved across the dry land to the river's bank, and was gone. Since that day I've refused to go fishing. My hooks are rusted, my lures unkempt. Some nights I make my way to the riverbank, and watch the water muscle past. Once or twice that fish came back. The tear in its cheek unhealed. Once or twice it hoisted itself above the water, and looked at me. I looked back. But I had nothing left to say.

IV

It's a short journey, but a hard one. The wind is up, the ferry grinding the surface of the sea. All the green pales to white, little boats scuttle out of range. We stand at the rail, almost touching. Below us the churn and bluster of the wake stretches out, a trench between island and port. Once, on this trip, dolphins rose up to observe us. If they do so this time, you will smile again. Like that day you turned to me, shining, when the whales called. Like that time we looked, properly, into the sea. After which you packed away all your hooks and rods. I should stay, of course I should, but I leave you alone at the rail.

V

The green skin of the sea. The slap of the waves against the stern. One slice of keel through the waves and the dolphins appear, shifty-eyed, trading truth for wit. A second slice, and here come the sharks, full steam and earnest. Below them the stingrays, thinking of nothing but air: they lift, and flow, and lift again, they rise toward the meniscus of the sea. You walk across the deck, pretending it's the sea. Still thinking you are Jesus. Look ahead, not down. Don't believe the depths.

VI

As the ferry struggled to the top of the swell we saw the city rise up out of the sea. Its scent drizzled across the water, metal and lead. Sun was up, the roofs of the cars glittered like fish scales. The baby squealed to see it: squealed, and clapped his little hands. You looked away, impassive. Pinned between the ocean and the land. After the last storm, after the hours you spent spooling water onto beached waves, you broke your rods and sliced your nets. *This shining creature on shore*, you said to me, through regretted tears, *this dying world.* You turned away, silent.

VII

The boat is running, the wind hard behind us. The boom ricochets across the deck. Insouciant. It's already taken out three of the team but we go by the old ways. *If not duffers, won't drown.* And anyway there's no turning back. Someone tossed a life-ring overboard and in seconds it was out of sight. We should have shortened sail hours ago but it's too late now, no one's game to face the rigging, Captain is talking about shooting down the sail but that'll be the drink in him. Someone sober has a go at reefing, but we can't keep it steady, and then one of the shrouds snaps and just about takes off his arm. One hand for the ship and one hand for yourself. I hear the sound of praying. Much good that'll do us, here, between the devil and the deep. The compass has gone, the rudder is broken, the Captain is in his cups, and the boat keeps running, its timbers singing with the storm, it doesn't know to which port it is sailing, and it doesn't give a damn.

1973

He died when I was away from home, not knowing it would happen, not expecting that something so momentous could arrive without its having made an appointment, but he did anyway die, and me without my thoughts straight without my face on without the words to say ready on my tongue. The world is too big in his absence, it takes a week to cross the street a month to make that call. The world is too big and there is no space in it for all the words we failed to share.

Starting over

It has come to an end. It's not the choice you would have made but you've run out of choice. Put out the bins, wipe the counters clean. They are waiting for the keys to your house. Put your suitcase in the car. Take a last look round. In the park across the road, a goanna ambles past, unconcerned. Birds crash and thump through the trees, as they always have. Plovers, curlews, once an eagle that sent small birds into urgent conference. You look at your phone. No one has called to wish you well. How can you just leave, how could anyone? How can you imagine starting again, in another country?

What happened that night

It was my favourite dress, the one my sister gave me when her tastes moved on. A nipped-in waist, cut-down bodice, deep lace. I looked, in its folds, almost grown. I thought I'd always look that way. But the dress knew better. That it, like me, was grass. That the end of things would be tissue paper and a box, and then at last a hole in the ground. I thought otherwise, but the world keeps forgetting me; it notices me for a second, and then again it gazes into the glass. I don't reflect; I am not interesting. Time has lost interest too: it curls in on itself, running its fingers up and down its own folds, neglectful. The dress lost its glamour before I did. Last time I saw it, it was walking down the alley, walking away, not looking back.

Keeping the record straight

If the north had stood beside us. If, turning to walk away, you had only said. If the north would unbend, just a little. A moment lost, and another. If I had seized. Made the right or any moves. If the north turned to south. Agreed to disagree. If the north would stretch out its hand. Or buy a copy of my book. If just once; then never again this.

En route

Nine p.m., Terminal 2, Sydney airport. The doors are closed, the gate lounges thrum, security guards watch us edgily, and in all the talk is the rise and fall of someone practising scales. We can't be certain we're alive. The clocks have stopped. The barista has gone home. Even the air smells of dead feet. Seagulls are larking about outside: this is their day. He peers out through the window but there's no sign of sky. Slowly, self-consciously, he touches his tongue to the glass. It tastes of other people's hands.

Icarus

When you said don't go I went anyway. Paid what I needed to pay. Nights in terror?—no matter. Things could always be worse. Ask the dolphins who romp alongside your boat, laughing. They have found the escape clause. They can tell a hawk from a handsaw, a tired chair from a tree. If they can, I can. Eels in the Sargasso, seagulls on the wing. Watch me fly.

Waiting for the bus

I

It will come. Sometimes it comes early, leaving you breathless on the footpath. Other times it's late, arriving after you had given up hope. This erratic life. The phone won't ring, and then it does, and sometimes it's you saying *hello? hello?* One day I'll reply, another day I leave the phone on the table and walk away. Yes of course I'll regret it once the moment passes. But it hasn't passed yet.

II

I am waiting for the bus. It runs later each day, as though time were running out, as though time had lost its way. The roads too are running out, fading from the maps, and the GPS on your car scans wildly, Karen's or Leigh's or Serena's machine voice growing ever more anxious. These things happen; remember that year when the old mines gave way on the Rand, and small towns vanished? The nation mourned; the miners kept mining. We need to wait better.

III

We met at the bus stop when he sat beside me, uncomfortably close. His alien thigh warm along mine, shoulder against shoulder. He wore women's tights, brightly patterned, and shoes that sparkled fairy lights. We could have been a pair, Mr and Mrs on a Wetterhaus, salt and pepper in an Art Deco cruet. When he breathed against my ear I took fright. If it happens again, I'll stay.

IV

The bus took Brendan, its mirror catching him just at the temple, and he died very quietly, there at the bus stop, ironically below the warning signs, while the bus driver howled, and pedestrians covered their mouths helplessly, and the sirens drew closer, their cries shuttering the space.

V

When she stood up to summon the bus a scrap of paper fluttered from her bag. *Milk*, it read. *Tissues. Firewood. Another chance.* The bus stopped; she stepped aboard.

VI

I am waiting for the bus. Three have wandered past, none of them mine. I should light a cigarette: an invocation to the gods. Silence swells between us. I never speak your name but you are in everything I say.

VII

A bus pulls up at my stop but it's the wrong one. I stay put. Minutes crawl by. All that breath circulating in the space between black road and blue sky. All that life. Traffic builds on both sides of the street, the cars go past, the minutes pass, children pass me on their way to school. On the wall of the shelter someone has scrawled a Jesus. The empty tomb, the forgotten bones. Your place is empty without you. In your absence its edges blur.

VIII

It happens just like that: you are planning next week's lunch; reading the minutes of the meeting; about to call your secret lover. Everything changes. You are just choosing the right golf club for your next swing, have just flicked on the indicator as you prepare to turn the corner into your street, you're reaching for the phone. You are balancing your cheque account, demanding to speak to the manager, stepping out to feed the magpies. It matters so much less than you'd imagined. Sure your lover will be temporarily bereft, but someone else will chair the meeting, play the ball. It will all go on, while you will not, while you drift like smoke into history.

Drops in time

Trace a line past the sneezing guard to the far room. Drifting from the underbellies of sacks there's nutmeg, cinnamon, cloves. The floor is turned to gold. Cardamon and caraway ground fine, turmeric and fenugreek—'for a bit of an edge', says the shopkeeper, eyes streaming. The air is turned to scent. Paprika and galangal, a touch of lemongrass. As though someone were cooking, too much, too near. Cassia, and cumin. Star anise, settled on my skin. Taste me, breathe me in. We are drops in time. I stand, poised, on the edge of the wave. A cloud filters the light, someone's washing is on the line. It will need to be washed again.

from Ernesto Neto, 'Just like drops in time, nothing' (2002), Art Gallery of New South Wales.

Da capo

When the air is soft, and the sun sits perfectly on the horizon, and the neighbour's boy opens his window so the voice of his cello washes against the fence. When the magpies sing for their supper, and the marigolds store the light of the sun against the night hours. Inside the house right now it's all prowling, and voices that crack and fall. Inside is all shudder, and you need to sign that form and you find that dammit you've bought only purple garlic, not white, and the cat has trapped herself in the cupboard again, and no one has emptied the bin. Breathe. It's easily fixed. You pass out drinks, and comfort the cat, and calm comes in with the evening light, and the sun sets, perfectly, and night curls itself around the house.

Afterword

For Jacques Derrida, the etymology of the word 'archive' directs attention to two distinct principles: the sequential and the jussive. In this way it references not only the where and the when of an event, but also the systems and buildings that contain, organise and preserve its record. In its sequential identity, the archive is simply an historical repository; in the jussive, it is political authority, archive that shapes the future through the way it records the past.

I named this collection *Sentences from the Archive* because I have long been wrestling with the ways in which creative practice can operate in the political zone. In an article published in 2009, my concern was with the narratives that 'produced' the ways of knowing the crisis that was 11 September 2001. Now I shift my focus to small individual crises and memories, and am trying to think my way into how a person, no less than a nation, might construct archives, and make sense of the past, in the work of facing and building the future.

I use prose poems because they obey the logic of the sentence rather than the line. I sense that the expressive sentence may trump the jussive sentence: that which confines individuals and communities within the prisonhouse of authorised memory. And I am looking for a more fluid, more playful and more 'generous' way (to use Mitchell Whitelaw's term) to access what has already been tagged and lodged in one's personal archive; because what has been told—if it is retrievable—can be told again, and told better.

> Derrida, Jacques (1995) 'Archive Fever: A Freudian Impression' (translated by Eric Prenowitz), *Diacritics* 25.2.
>
> Webb, Jen (2009) 'Sentences from the Archives', *Performance Paradigm* 5.1.
>
> Whitelaw, Mitchell (2015) 'Generous Interfaces for Digital Cultural Collections', *Digital Humanities Quarterly* 9.1.

Acknowledgments

The poems in this collection were all presented in draft form to the Prose Poetry Project that was initiated, and is still managed, by the International Poetry Studies Institute at the University of Canberra. My thanks to all the members of the PPP who accept whatever comes their way, generate new ways of thinking, seeing and doing, and provide unstinting support even for the silliest of attempts to craft a new poem. Particular thanks to Shane Strange, preferred publisher of our outputs. Much of the thinking and investigation that led to these poems emerged from research funded by the Australian Research Council for Discovery Project #130100402, 'Understanding Creative Excellence: A Case Study in Poetry'.

Jen Webb is a writer and cultural theorist, and Director at the Centre for Creative and Cultural Reasearch at the University of Canberra. She writes poetry, researches creative practive and makes and exhibits artists' books. Her most recent books are *Watching the World* (Blemish Books, 2015), *Researching Creative Writing* (Frontinus, 2015) and *Art and Human Rights: Contemporary Asian Contexts* (Manchester University Press).

More Recent Work

Owen Bullock — *Urban Haiku (2015)*
River's Edge (2016)

Paul Hetherington — *Gallery of Antique Art (2016)*

Niloofar Fanaiyan — *Transit (2016)*

Prose Poetry Project — *Pulse (2016)*

Jen Webb — *Sentences from the Archive (2016)*

Monica Carroll, Jen Crawford, Owen Bullock & Shane Strange — *5 6 7 8 (2016)*

Subjash Jaireth — *Incantations (2016)*

all titles available from
www.recentworkpress.com

www.ingramcontent.com/pod-product-compliance
Ingram Content Group UK Ltd.
Pitfield, Milton Keynes, MK11 3LW, UK
UKHW041301180426
11947UKWH00009B/611